Introduction

Here comes the plane now! I can hardly wait to meet my aunt and uncle—and my four cousins! I was born in Canada and my family has lived here for fourteen years! Now my relatives are immigrating here and will be staying with our family until they can find a place of their own. I wonder what they will be like. Will my cousins want to do the same things I do? Will they like our food? I wonder what grade they're in.

New immigrants at Toronto International Airport

1. Thousands of people immigrate to Canada each year. Write down what you think is the meaning of the word "immigrant". Check your definition with that of a dictionary.

2. Using construction paper, make a cover for your booklet *Canada: Land of Immigrants* in which you can keep a record of your findings. Pictures, drawings, and paintings will make your cover more interesting.

3. On our street there are O'Neils whose ancestors came to Canada from Ireland in 1832, Pelletiers who immigrated to Canada from France in 1967, Arkevelds who came from Holland to Canada in 1924, and Dhillons who came to Canada from India in 1956. Try to discover when your ancestors first came to Canada and from what country they immigrated. Is there anyone living in Canada today whose ancestors never immigrated to Canada from another country?

1

Imagine yourself as one of those people aboard a plane coming to settle in Canada. Before making your decision to leave your own country, there were many questions you had to have answered, many decisions you had to make.

1. Join together with several other students. Decide in what country your group is now living — it could be anywhere from Bolivia in South America, to Italy, Germany, or even India. Come to some decision on your reasons for wanting to emigrate from your own country. What would you want to know about Canada before deciding to immigrate here? Add as many questions as you can to this list.

What is the climate like?
What jobs are available?
What is Canada's immigration policy?
What are the educational opportunities?
What are the people like?
Do we have any friends or relatives in Canada?
What type of government do they have?
Is there any discrimination against people from our country in Canada?

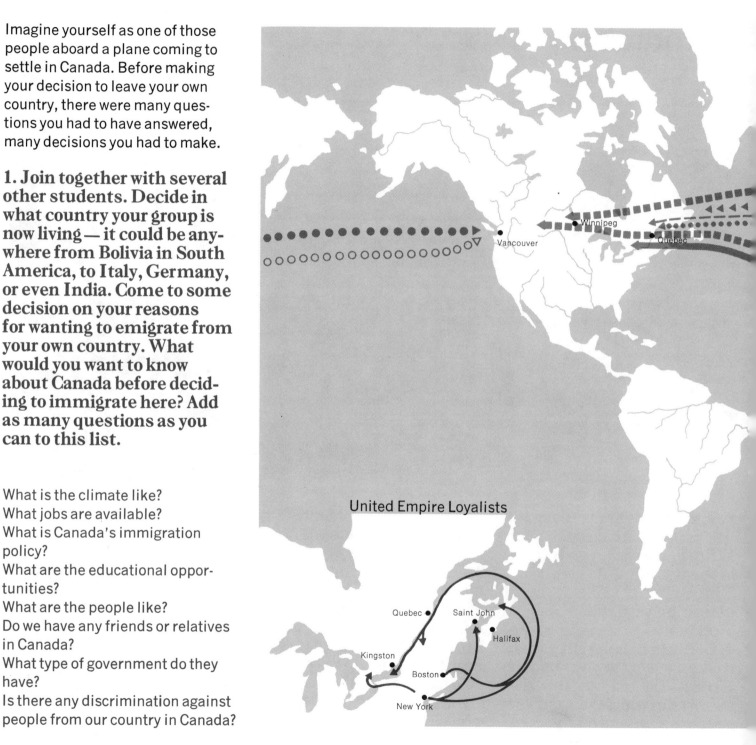

United Empire Loyalists

2

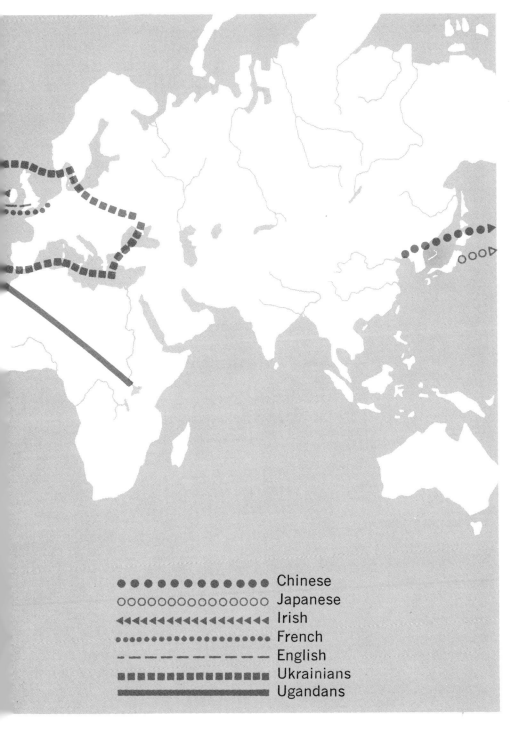

●●●●●●●●●●●●	Chinese
○○○○○○○○○○○○	Japanese
◄◄◄◄◄◄◄◄◄◄◄◄◄◄	Irish
•••••••••••••••••	French
– – – – – – – – – –	English
■■■■■■■■■■■■■■	Ukrainians
▬▬▬▬▬▬▬▬	Ugandans

2. Where would a person intending to immigrate to Canada acquire all of this information?

3. In a group, select a chairman to direct activities. Each student should research two or three of the questions which would concern a person considering immigrating to Canada. Together write up your answers in the form of an Information Handbook for immigrants.

Canada has immigration officers in many different countries. These people provide pamphlets, information, and immigration forms to people wishing to move to Canada.

1. If you were an immigration officer, what questions would you ask a family before allowing them to come to Canada?

2. Is everyone who applies to immigrate to Canada allowed to do so? How do you think the Canadian government decides? Can you think of any type of person that the government would not like to bring to Canada? What type of person would the government be anxious to encourage?

WHO CAN COME TO CANADA?

Anyone may apply to come to Canada and applicants will be judged by the same standards in every area of the world.

There are three categories of immigrants and your first step should be to determine which category covers your relative:

SPONSORED DEPENDANTS
NOMINATED RELATIVES
INDEPENDENT APPLICANTS

You, as a Canadian citizen or permanent resident of Canada, are entitled to "SPONSOR" your dependants or to apply to "NOMINATE" other relatives.

Your "sponsorship" can assure that your dependant will qualify for admission to Canada if he is in good health and of good character.

Your "nomination" will greatly assist the application of a non-dependant relative when he is examined by an Immigration Officer overseas.

HOW TO DETERMINE YOUR RELATIVE'S GROUP

A "SPONSORED DEPENDANT" is:

— a husband or wife
— an unmarried son or daughter under twenty-one
— a fiancé or fiancée
— a parent or grandparent aged sixty or older
— a parent or grandparent under sixty if widowed or unable to work
— orphans under 18 in the following categories: grandchild, brother, sister, nephew or niece
— the nearest relative in cases where the applicant has no living dependant other than husband or wife. (An applicant can sponsor only one relative in this way.)

The application for a "Sponsored Dependant" also covers any members of the dependant's immediate family who would be entering Canada with him. "Immediate family" under the immigration regulations means husband or wife and any unmarried sons or daughters under 21.

A "NOMINATED RELATIVE" is:

— an unmarried son or daughter twenty-one years or over
— a married son or daughter under twenty-one
— a brother or sister
— a parent or grandparent under sixty years
— a nephew, niece, uncle, aunt or grandchild

In each case the application covers those members of the immigrant's immediate family who would accompany him to Canada.

AN "INDEPENDENT APPLICANT" is:

— anyone who does not come into any of the above classes of relatives, or anyone else who applies for admission to Canada.

WHAT IS YOUR RESPONSIBILITY?

In applying to sponsor or nominate a relative, you are taking an important step, both for yourself and your family in Canada, and for your relatives overseas. You should, therefore, make yourself familiar with the responsibility you are undertaking in helping a relative re-establish in Canada.

In the case of a sponsored dependant, you are assuming full responsibility for his support. For a nominated relative, you are accepting responsibility for care, accommodation, maintenance, and assistance in locating employment, if required, for a period of up to five years.

THE "INDEPENDENT APPLICANT"

An independent applicant will be examined abroad in much the same way as a nominated relative. His application will be considered on the same factors of education, personal qualities, occupational demand, age and occupational skill, plus four additional factors.

These are whether he has a job arranged in Canada, whether he has a knowledge of English or French or both, whether he has a relative willing to help him get established and whether employment opportunities are good or poor in his area of destination.

If the relative you wish to bring to Canada does not meet the definition of either a nominated relative or a sponsored dependant, he may still apply in his own right at a Canadian Immigration Visa Office overseas for admission as an independent immigrant.

VISITORS

It sometimes happens that a relative comes to Canada to visit and then decides that he or she would like to stay as an immigrant.

In the case of SPONSORED DEPENDANTS, this makes no difference. You apply in the same way, your relative will be interviewed by an immigration officer in Canada, and he or she will be given immigrant status providing the requirements of the Immigration Act and Regulations are met.

If you apply to NOMINATE a non-dependant relative, the same procedure will be followed; but if he is in Canada your nomination will NOT assist the application to the same large extent as if the relative were still abroad.

In other words, it is better for a nominated relative that you should apply for him as an immigrant in the first place, not have him come to Canada as a visitor. That reduces his chances of being accepted.

Ottawa, 1968

You are considering sponsoring someone to come to Canada to live. Write a brief answer to the following questions which had puzzled you before you read this pamphlet published by the Department of Manpower and Immigration in Ottawa.
● Why does the immigration department establish a category system for new immigrants?
● How can you justify the government's action that compels an individual who sponsors or nominates a relative to be responsible for the "care, accommodation, and maintenance" of that relative for a period of five years?
● In November 1972 the section of the pamphlet on visitors was suspended. Can you explain why?
● Examine your local newspapers to discover items which might suggest why some Canadians might not welcome new immigrants.

The Globe and Mail, Toronto

5

Let us trace the case of a typical immigrant, Hans Wieland, a motor mechanic from Germany, as he considers emigrating to Canada with his wife and two children. What will he have to do? How will he and his family be "processed"?

"He will probably start off by writing to the Canadian Immigration Office, Stuttgart, (there are five such offices in Germany) stating his wish to emigrate and asking for information on how he should proceed. The Canadian Immigration Office will send him an application form, requesting that he fill it out and send it back. The form includes such questions as name, place and date of birth, ethnic origin, marital status, date and place of marriage and maiden name of wife, present citizenship and present occupation, and relationship of dependents. It enquires as to whether there has been any criminal offence or conviction, some general questions on the health of the applicant and his family; whether he has been in Canada previously and if so when; whether he can pay for his passage to Canada; whether he will need some assistance with passage; and how much money he intends to transfer to Canada. It asks if he had friends, relatives or employers in Canada, and who they are, and also how soon he and his

family would be prepared to leave for Canada. It has a section on languages, on education, on practical training. It asks for passport particulars and for former addresses and employment since 1939. It is, in fact, a fairly comprehensive two-page questionnaire, not unlike, in many respects, application forms for employment or for insurance.

"When the Canadian Immigration Office receives the completed questionnaire they will write to Mr. Wieland requesting that he and his family go to Stuttgart on a certain day, or, if this is not possible, that he suggest another day more convenient for them all. Upon arrival there, he and each member of his family will be given a thorough physical examination including chest X-ray. Following this he will be interviewed by one of the Immigration Officers, when as much as possible will be learned of what he hopes for in Canada—place, type of employment, social amenities, and so forth—while at the same time information about conditions in Canada will be given to him, including some printed material in his own language. At this time the question of assisted passage will also be discussed—whether he can pay his own passage or whether he will need some assistance from the Canadian Government in the form

of a loan. At this time also he must produce and leave with the Canadian Immigration authorities a certificate from the German police and his passport. Prior to this, upon receipt of his application form, his qualifications will have been examined and some of his references followed up. Following this interview he will be told that he will hear shortly from the Immigration Office.

"While here he will also be interviewed by a Canadian security officer.

"When all the information has been gathered—general information, employment, skills and experience, health and security—a decision will be made to accept or

reject his application. In either case he will be notified.

"If his application is accepted he will be asked to book his passage and to send in a receipt or a letter or some other evidence of having done so. Upon receipt of this information the Canadian Immigration Office will send him his passport and visa and he is then free to make final arrangements to proceed to Canada."

(From *New Roots in Canadian Soil* by J. P. Kidd)

With a partner, imagine that one of you is the newly arrived immigrant and the other is the Canadian reporter waiting at the airport. Conduct an "on-the-spot" interview. Make up the dialogue, but try to make the situation sound as authentic as possible. You may wish to use a tape recorder and later present your interview to the class.

How are immigrants received once they arrive in Canada? Here is how the Ontario government welcomes new arrivals.

The red carpet welcome Ontario gives immigrants at airport

In his elegant blazer with the Ontario crest on the pocket, Peter Solly-Flood looks like a successful tour director.

He is the kind of man you would be glad to find in charge of the trip that is going to take you through 11 European countries in 10 days: friendly yet authoritative, jovial but tough-minded.

And, in a way, that is what his job is, except that his territory isn't Europe or South America—just several hundred square feet of glass and stainless steel jungle in the immigration area of Toronto International Airport.

As head of the Ontario Department of Citizenship's airport reception services, the tour he takes you through is a series of desks, corridors and offices.

When you start, you are a nervous immigrant, just off the plane, not knowing what to expect in this strange world of rooms with rows of black chairs facing nothing in particular and corridors where all the doors seem to be marked private.

When you finish, you are usually weeping and in the arms of your fiancee or your mother in the mad scramble of the airport arrivals hall.

In the meantime, you have become a landed immigrant, found your luggage, cleared customs, received documentation about everything from OHSIP to workmens' compensation and been wished good luck at least four times.

For any traveller who knows what it is like to be unilingual and luggage-less in Beirut or who has tangled with a telephone in Zagreb, the service is like a dream.

It combines everything you have always secretly wanted your arrival in a strange place to be like. In Canada, it happens only once—on that very first arrival as a new Canadian—and it is almost worth emigrating just to get the treatment.

The service has been operating at Toronto since last May and it starts about 30 seconds after you leave the plane.

You walk down a corridor and you see a girl in a mauve uniform—either a pantsuit or a mididress—who looks like an airline hostess except that the gold badge on her breast says simply Ontario.

"Immigrants this way," she says, with a smile, pointing to one of the glass-partitioned segments of the great hall. "Tourists and returning residents straight on."

Tourists and returning residents would eat their hearts out if they knew what they were missing: the services of Mr. Solly-Flood (available in French, German and Serbo-Croat) and his three assistants: Tatiana Lehner-Benzaquen (Italian, Spanish, Serbo-Croat), Irene Szalowski (Polish, Russian, Italian) and Veria Mancini (Spanish, Italian, Portuguese).

What sets Reception Services apart from similar organizations around the world is that it is not just an information desk.

For example, most immigrants are met by relatives. Reception services will ask you if there is someone there to take care of you once you have cleared customs. But if you have language problems or seem unsure, they won't simply take your word for it.

Tatiana, Irene or Veria will go with you to peer through the glass screen so you can scan the crowds thronging outside the customs area until you see a familiar face.

1. If you were coming to Canada to live, would you appreciate the services provided by the Ontario government? What do you suppose might happen if you were an immigrant and there was no one to greet you on your arrival in Canada? How would you feel?
2. What services are still lacking?

3. How do you suppose the arrival of an immigrant today differs from that of an immigrant arriving 100 or 200 years ago?

Today, jobs and a higher standard of living are two factors that make Canada appear very attractive to immigrants. But Canada has always been a "land of immigrants". What factors have encouraged people from so many different countries to emigrate to Canada through the centuries to make it the country it is today? Three case studies should help us in our investigation and give us some insight into immigration in Canada's past.

If there is no one there, they will help you get in touch with someone, a process that may take five minutes or 10 hours.

Since May, the entry of more than 12,000 immigrants to Canada has been smoothed by reception services and the only serious criticism of the service has come from Mr. Solly-Flood himself. It doesn't go far enough, doesn't extend outside the airport.

"What we need most," he says, "is an office downtown where the immigrants can come back to us once they start to tackle the real problems of settling in."

The Department of Citizenship is currently studying a proposal for extending the service into the city to provide a follow-up. For the moment, the service is strictly a short idyll in the life of the immigrant: he may never have it so easy again.

The Globe and Mail, Toronto, Jan. 1972

(MTL3) MONTREAL, SEPT 28--ON HIS KNEE--Bryce Mackasay smiles as he sets on his knee two Ugandan children, part of a group which arrived at Montreal International airport Thursday. Mr. Mackasay, along with other government officials, was on hand to greet the arrivals. (CP WIRE CT 1972(STP-MG)MG8a--SEE WIRESTORY--

The Loyalists

Bitter feelings raged from the outset of the American Revolution in 1776 until long after its end in 1783. Neighbours in the Thirteen Colonies became fierce enemies as some sided with the revolutionists wanting independence from England; others vowed to remain loyal to England and the King.

Loyalists faced persecution from the revolutionists; their lands and homes were seized and many faced the humiliation of being tarred, feathered, and run out of town.

By mid 1783, 100,000 Loyalists had left the United States. Britain and the British West Indies were the destination of some, but many chose the areas of present-day Nova Scotia, New Brunswick, the Eastern Townships of Quebec, and southern Ontario.

1. Why are the Loyalists on page 11 using tents rather than building cabins?
2. About how many people would be in this travelling party? What would be some advantages of travelling in a large group? Why might it be safer to travel through the United States to Canada in

a small group at this time?
3. How do you think the life of the Loyalists as shown in this picture compares with their life before the outbreak of the War of Independence? Choose one of the characters in this sketch and write his letter to a friend or relative in England describing recent events in his life.

Michael Grass was a Loyalist in 1783. This account was related many years later by his son, John, to Reverend James Richardson, who wrote it down in 1862.

My father, Michael Grass, lived, at the breaking out of the Revolutionary War, on a farm about 30 miles above New York. He was a native of Germany, but had lived most of his time in America. When the Revolu-tion commenced General Herkimer sent my father an invitation to join the Americans and offered him a Captain's Commission. My father replied:—"I have sworn allegiance to one King and I cannot serve any other." For this saying he was driven from his home and family and was obliged to take refuge within the British lines at New York. His family followed shortly afterwards. He lost his farm and property and

Encampment of the Loyalists at New Johnstown (Cornwall), St. Lawrence River, 1784

was obliged to maintain his family at New York by working as a harness maker. At the close of the War the British General commanding at New York, having heard that my father had been a prisoner of the French at Frontenac, in the time of the old French War, sent for him to enquire about the place and said:—"Mr. Grass, I understand that you have been at Frontenac in Canada. What sort of a country is it? Can people live there?" My father replied: "What I saw of it, I think it a fine country, and if people were settled there, I think they would do very well." The Governor replied: "Oh Mr. Grass, I am delighted to hear you say so, for we don't know what to do with the poor Loyalists. The city is full of them and we cannot send them all to Nova Scotia. Would you be willing Mr. Grass to take charge of such as would be willing to go with you to Frontenac? If so I can furnish you a conveyance by ship to Quebec, and rations for you all until such time as you may have means to provide for yourselves."

My father asked for three days in which to make up his mind. At the end of the three days he accepted. Notices were then posted throughout the City calling upon all those who would go to Frontenac to enroll their names with Mr. Grass.

The Company of men, women and children having been completed, a

Loyalists on their way to Upper Canada, 1784

ship was provided and furnished, and they started for the unknown and distant region, leaving behind them homes and friends of their youth, never probably to see them again; the fruits of all their former toils and sufferings being thus sacrificed on the altar of their loyalty.

The first season they got no further than Sorel in lower Canada where they were obliged to erect log huts for shelter during the winter. The next spring they took boats and proceeded up the St. Lawrence, at last reached Frontenac and pitched

their tents on Indian Point where the Marine Docks at Kingston now stand. Here they awaited the survey of the townships which was not accomplished so as to have the lots ready for location before July.

1. Historians, when they are trying to reconstruct the past, search out information from primary and secondary sources. What do you think these terms mean? Is the Grass story a primary

12

source? If not, why not? What are the dangers of such an account? How would you protect yourself against the dangers you have listed?

2. Prior to the outbreak of the Revolutionary War, where did Grass live? Why had he joined the British forces? At what price? Why had the British General of New York requested Grass's comments on the type of land around Cataraqui (Frontenac)? Where else were the Loyalists to be sent? What was Grass's role to be concerning the Loyalist settlement at Cataraqui (Frontenac)? Why did they only reach Sorel the first year? How did they reach Frontenac the next year?

3. Suppose you had not joined Grass's company and had not received government assistance (assisted sea voyage), how might you have arrived at Cataraqui (Kingston)? Prepare an imaginary journey in the form of a log book or diary.

4. Compare the means of transportation used by people immigrating from the United States to Canada today with that used by the Loyalists.

Loyalists camping on their way up the St. Lawrence, 1784

The following excerpt, in Michael Grass' own words, describes the journey to Upper Canada.

We creep along day by day, fearful of every noise, every moving object. The revolutionists despise us and would gladly murder us as traitors. Soon we will reach British North

America. But, what will our lives be like there starting everything afresh?

I've heard it said that the trees grow so thick together there that it takes days before a clearing large enough for even a cabin can be cleared. Surely we will be rewarded for our loyalty to the King and will be provided with land, seed and implements?

But, what if this is not to be the case?

Just before we left our home in New York, we had news about my sister's family. They had fled a year earlier than we. A boat from New York City had landed their Loyalist party in Nova Scotia. I can hardly imagine the anxiety Clara and Stephen must have gone through as they waited their turn to draw the lot for their lands.

Loyalists drawing lots for their lands, 1784

1. You are Clara or Stephen about to draw your lot. Describe your feelings just before you cast your hand into the hat.

2. What do you suppose the man with the pen is doing? What is on the ground at his feet?

3. Do you think these Loyalists are paying for their land? Why would Britain be willing to give these people free lands?

The first Loyalists to the Maritime Provinces (called Nova Scotia in those days) arrived by sea at Halifax from New York. Their first need was to find shelter from the approaching winter. Governor Parr lent his assistance to this need. As the Loyalists sought out new homes throughout Nova Scotia, they began to complain about the lack of support from Parr and the British government. Growing out of the complaints a decision was reached to establish two new provinces—

Cape Breton and New Brunswick. Approximately 30,000 new settlers were added to the Maritime Provinces by the influx of Loyalists.

1. Prepare an outline map of the Maritime Provinces. Mark on the following: Halifax, Saint John, St. John River, Fredericton, Bay of Fundy, Cape Breton Island, Annapolis Valley, and Shelburne.

2. Suppose the Loyalists established settlements along the St. John River, on Cape Breton Island and in the Annapolis Valley. What do you think would be some of the major problems facing the governor of the day?

Col. Thomas Dundas to Earl Cornwallis, from Saint John, December 28, 1786.

My Colleague and I, after having finished the business of our commission at Halifax, visited all the different settlements of Nova Scotia, which surpass anything I could expect to have seen in a climate which has seven months winter. The new settlements made by the Loyalists are in a thriving way, although rum and idle habits contracted during the war are much against them. They have experienced every possible injury from the old inhabitants of Nova Scotia, who are even more disaffected towards the British Government than any of the new States ever were. . . .

In the month of October we came to the province where we found very different principles. Mr. Carleton by his own attention and firmness, assisted by a well chosen council, has established good government. The province contains all that part of Nova Scotia which lies to the westward of the Bay of Fundy. It con-tains good lands, the farmers who have fled from the States are well pleased with the soil. The number of the Loyalists is 12,000. The old inhabitants are not 3,000 and these are a despicable race ready to sell their improvements as the Loyalists are enabled to purchase from them.

1. Col. Dundas has just completed a tour of the Loyalist settlements. Why were the Loyalists living in New Brunswick more successful than the Loyalists in Nova Scotia?
2. In New Brunswick the ratio of Loyalists to former inhabitants was 4 :1. What seemed to be the relationship between the Loyalists and the former inhabitants of New Brunswick?
3. Do you know of any cases where immigrants have not been treated fairly by the inhabitants of your community?

Simeon Perkins, a merchant, settled in Liverpool, Nova Scotia, in the early 1760s. For a long time, he missed his many friends from Boston, where he had formerly lived. At least once every two years, he returned with one of his schooner captains to Boston to spend three weeks with his former friends. Between trips he relied on an exchange of letters to the many New England captains who stopped at Liverpool to exchange their goods and replenish their supplies.

1. Locate Liverpool in your atlas.
2. How far is Liverpool from Halifax and Boston?
3. New England immigrants to Nova Scotia were often called pre-Loyalists. To whom would they be loyal during the American Revolutionary War?
4. Your answer to (3) might indicate that during wartime certain groups of immigrants might pose a problem to your country.
(a) Can you list the names of other groups of immigrants that might have posed a problem to the Canadian prime minister of the day?
(b) Suppose you were the Canadian prime minister, what would you recommend that your government do to deal with such situations?
(c) Suppose you were the new immigrant faced with the situation suggested in (b), what would your attitude be towards the prime minister and your new country?

The Irish

Some of you "United Empire Loyalists" don't even know what it's like to suffer. At least you had it pretty good in the Thirteen Colonies before the War. I've never had it good.

By the time I had finally scraped together enough money to leave Ireland and come to British North America, I had nearly starved to death. The population there was increasing rapidly and the majority of the people lived in misery on nothing but potatoes. No fat turkey ever graced our bare tables!

Absentee landlords ordered their fawning agents to wring all they could from the impoverished tenants, and when disorders among the tenants became widespread, why they simply evicted us—threw us into the streets.

In 1817-19, famine and fever ravished the population and the failure of the potato crop in 1821 because of too much rain made thievery common place. We were forced to steal in order to feed our children, let alone keep ourselves alive. In 1822, the shortage of potatoes caused the price to quadruple and millions were practically reduced to starvation.

The quotation below from the *Edinburgh Review*, December 1826, describes the life of the Irish at this time.

"Those who have never travelled in Ireland can form but a very imperfect idea of the distress that generally pervades that unhappy country. Often have I seen in one miserable, nearly unroofed dwelling, with scarcely a window remaining, from ten to twelve, *and in some instances more,* families, pent up together, with not an article of household furniture save the shattered remains of an old oak table, or a solitary chair without a back, or a broken stool. And for culinary utensils an iron pot not unfrequently serves the three-fold purposes of tea kettle, *if they are able to raise the tea,* a pot to boil the potatoes in, or stirabout, *meat they have none,* and a vessel to wash the tattered remains of their wretched garments in; these, with *perhaps* a broken cup and saucer, make up the sum of the whole of their moveable effects. In every street and alley are to be seen groups of human beings in a state of half nudity; women with their almost lifeless infants struggling to obtain a portion of the scanty nutriment from their exhausted mothers, while their reckless and infuriated fathers wander the streets, lost to all hope, and maddened with hunger and despair. Nay, I have frequently seen women with the lifeless bodies of their infant children in their arms, prowling from street to street, and begging from the casual passengers the means of depositing the remains of their departed offspring in the grave!"

Arrivals at the Port of Quebec from the British Isles 1829-1859

From England: ————————
From Ireland: — — — — — — —
From Scotland: ··············

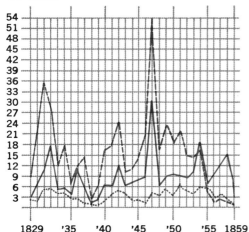

Thousands

1829 '35 '40 '45 '50 '55 1859

Ejection of the Irish tenantry

Interior of an Irish peasant's cottage

1. If you were one of the figures in these pictures would you have wanted to immigrate to Canada? Why? Why might some of the Irish have wanted to stay in Ireland? Why could not everyone who wanted to leave Ireland for Canada do so?

2. Imagine yourself as the provider for the starving children in these pictures. Would you steal to keep them from starving? Would this be right or wrong?

3. You are a reporter. Write a newspaper article to describe a day in the life of a typical poor Irish family at this time.

1. **What might happen if the stowaways were discovered?**
2. **Why would they risk such dangers?**
3. **Suppose you were a captain of an immigrant ship, what might you do if you discovered a destitute immigrant stowaway?**

Many destitute men, unable to scrape together enough money for a fare, passed days or weeks hidden in barrels or chests aboard ships bound for Canada. They were often more dead than alive when discovered.

Often those who could save enough money to sail to Canada were little better off than those who tried to stow away on the ships.

The search for stowaways

18

Search these pictures for clues about conditions aboard immigrant ships. Make several generalizations stating what you consider these conditions to have been like. Then read this account written in 1874 to test your generalizations to see if they are correct.

On board an immigrant ship in the thirties

Hundreds of poor people, men, women, and children; of all years from the drivelling idiot of 90 to the babe just born; huddled together without light, without air; wallowing in filth and breathing a foetid atmosphere; sick in body; dispirited in heart;—the fevered Patients lying between the Sound, in sleeping places so narrow as almost to deny them the power of indulging by a change of position the natural restlessness of the disease; by their agonized ravings disturbing those around, & predisposing them through the Effects of the imagination, to imbibe the contagion; living without food or medicine except as Administered by the hand of Casual charity; dying without the voice of Spiritual Consolation; and buried in the deep— without the rites of the Church. The food is generally ill selected and seldom sufficiently cooked in consequence of the insufficiency and bad construction of the cooking places. The supply of water hardly enough for cooking and drinking does not allow Washing. In many Ships the filthy beds teeming with all abominations are never required to be brought on Deck and aired;— the narrow space between the Sleeping berths & the piles of Boxes is never washed or scraped: but breathes up a damp and foetid stench, until the day before arrival at Quarantine when all hands are required to "Scrub Up",

and put on a fair face for the Doctor and Government Inspector. No moral restraint is attempted —the voice of prayer is never heard;— drunkenness and its consequence train of ruffianly debasement is not discouraged, because it is profitable to the Captain who traffics in the Grog. . . .

In addition to hunger, sickness and death by such dread diseases as cholera, the immigrant was also never free from the fear of shipwreck.

Ninety-six Irish immigrants aboard the *Barque Edmund* were drowned in 1850 when the ship crashed on rocks.

Who was responsible for the suffering, hardships, and deaths of the Irish immigrants? Was it the immigrant himself for deciding to emigrate to Canada? Was it the shipowner who allowed the Irish to live in such terrible conditions aboard his ship? Was it the Irish government for not making conditions better in Ireland so that citizens would not have to leave their own country? Or, was it the fault of the government in British North America who allowed or encouraged the Irish to come? Consider each possibility, then decide who you think was responsible. Join together with several other students to compare your decisions.

If they were able to survive the passage from Ireland to Canada, the immigrant had still not reached the end of his troubles. This account written in 1850 by a Quebec City doctor indicates the first view of Canada for many Irish.

These poor creatures, on landing, creep into any hovel they can, with all their foul things about them. When they are so numerous as to figure in the streets, they are put, I believe by the Colonial Government, into dilapidated houses, with something like rations, of which latter the worthier portion of the emigrants are apt to see but little: they are clutched by the clamorous.

The filthy and crowded state of the houses, the disgusting scenes going on in them, can only be guessed by a very bold imagination. I have trod the floor of one of such houses, almost over shoes in churned and sodden garbage, animal and vegetable. It required dissecting-room nerves to bear it.

After starving about Quebec for months, the helpless Irishman and

his family begin to creep up the country on charity or government aid, and thus strew the colony with beggary and disease.

The Wreck of the Barque Edmund

1. What happens to the Irish immigrant upon his arrival?
2. What does the government do to help these people?

3. What are conditions like in the government houses?
4. What eventually happens to the Irish immigrant?

5. Refer to such articles as "Ugandan Asians Overwhelmed by Welcome" (*Globe and Mail,* Septem-

ber 29, 1972) for a description of how some of our more recent immigrants arrived in Canada. Compare their arrival with that of the Irish.

6. Would the Irish have been able to use either of the modes of transportation advertised here? Why? What other means of transportation were being used at this time?

7. Transportation and communications have changed a lot since the days of the Irish immigration. Describe some of the changes and explain how they assist or hinder new immigrants arriving in Canada.

FOR CHAMBLY.—The STEAMER CHAMBLY will leave MONTREAL for CHAMBLY on WEDNESDAY AFTER-NOON, MAY 9, at FOUR o'clock.

Cabin Passage, 12s. 6d.—Steerage do. 6s. 3d.
May 3, 1832.

THE UPPER CANADA COACHES leave MONTREAL EVERY DAY except *Saturday* and *Sunday*, at FOUR o'clock, A.M.
Montreal, May 3, 1832.   d

LAKE ONTARIO.

THE SPLENDID NEW STEAMBOAT
GREAT BRITAIN,
CAPTAIN JOS. WHITNEY,
Propelled by two low pressure Engines, of 90 horse power each.

THE Public are respectfully informed that the following arrangements have been made for the months of APRIL, MAY and JUNE.

Will leave PRESCOTT every *Wednesday Morning,* commencing on the

18th April,	30th May,
25th April,	6th June,
2d May,	13th June,
9th May,	20th June,
16th May,	27th June.
23d May,	

Touching at BROCKVILLE, KINGSTON, COBOURG, PORT HOPE, YORK, and arrive at NIAGARA early on *Friday morning.*

Will leave NIAGARA every *Saturday* afternoon, at FIVE o'clock, commencing on

21st April,	2d June,
28th April,	9th June,
5th May,	16th June,
12th May,	23d June,
19th May,	30th June.
26th May,	

Calling at OSWEGO every *Sunday morning,* after 5th May next; also, KINGSTON, BROCKVILLE, and arrive at PRESCOTT on *Sunday evening.*

The Ladies' and Gentlemen's Cabins on board the *Great Britain* are finished in the same manner as the NEW YORK and LIVERPOOL Packet Ships, with State Rooms; and no expense has been spared in finishing and furnishing the Boat in the most comfortable manner; every endeavour will be used to accommodate Passengers, and ensure the greatest regularity.

N. B. Notice will be given of the arrangements for the months of July, August and September.
Prescott, U. C. April 9, 1832.

AN OFFICE has been established at PRESCOTT, U. C. for the LAKE ONTARIO STEAMBOATS, GREAT BRITAIN and QUEENSTON. Mr. MENEILLEY, the Agent, will at all times attend to the shipping of Articles to go by the above Boats; and every information will be given by him to Emigrants proceeding upwards.
April 9, 1832.

▲
The emigrant's welcome to Canada

1. Examine each of these cartoons on the immigration of this period. Try to discover what the cartoonists are trying to say. Why is the cartoonist mocking the immigrant for being lured to Canada by tales of free lands, timber, and grasslands?

2. Create a cartoon to illustrate a situation in which a modern-day immigrant feels he has been misled about opportunities in Canada because of what confronts him once he arrives in this country. Jobs, discrimination, or housing are possible topics.

Johnny Canuck leading immigrants in "The Maple Leaf Forever"

1. Who is the man conducting the singing supposed to represent?

2. What is the cartoonist trying to imply by picturing all of these people from different countries joining together under Johnny Canuck's leadership to sing ''The Maple Leaf Forever''?

3. Choose one nationality represented in the cartoon and discover the reasons for this group coming to Canada, when they came, where they settled, what contribution they have made to Canadian life and whether this group still comprises a large portion of Canada's immigration. If you choose a nationality that is well represented in your community, you can formulate a series of questions and then interview them.

The Ukrainians

Wilfrid Laurier

Clifford Sifton

In 1896, Sir Wilfrid Laurier was elected Prime Minister of Canada and the years from 1896 to 1911 brought great changes in the growing country. One of the greatest changes came about as the result of the appointment of Clifford Sifton as the Minister of Immigration.

The Laurier government believed that the key to prosperity for Canada lay in attracting immigration to settle Canada's West. Once settled, the West could provide the grain to feed the growing cities of the world. The settlers in turn would provide markets for the products of eastern Canada and would bring prosperity to the railroads by this increased trade.

But how to attract this immigration to Canada? Sifton launched into the campaign. Advertising placed in newspapers in Europe and the United States, as well as pamphlets and speakers crying the splendours of immigration to Canada, brought thousands to this country. Between 1897 and 1912 some 961,000 came to Canada from the British Isles, 784,000 crossed the border from the United States, and 594,000 immigrated from Europe. It was this latter group from Europe, with their national and religious ties—the Poles, Doukhobors, Germans, and Ukrainians—who gave the Canadian West some of its hardiest workers and its multi-cultural character.

1. Counting those from the British Isles, the United States, and Europe, how many immigrants came to Canada between 1897 and 1912?

2. Who was the man most responsible for the flood of immigration? Why?

3. Sifton once gave this description as a guide to the kind of people needed in the Canadian West: ''I think a stalwart peasant in a sheepskin coat, born on the soil, whose forefathers have been farmers for generations, with a stout wife and half a dozen children, is good quality.''

What does the remark ''born on the soil'' indicate about the immigrant's past? Why was there a need for many children at this time in the development of the Canadian West? Why would a stout wife be more useful than a frail one? Why do you think that Sifton wanted this type of immigrant? Do you

think he would have considered the Ukrainians pictured here as good quality immigrants? Why?

4. How do you think the development of the railroads at this time aided settlement of the West? How would it aid western prosperity once the immigrants were sufficiently settled to start to produce crops?

Map of Railways, early 20th Centu...

Why was there so much railway building around the turn of the century?

Date	Total railway mileage
1867	2,278
1900	17,657
1914	30,795

Canal Improvements

Rebuilding and widening commenced in the 1870s, but most work was done around the turn of the century. Why?

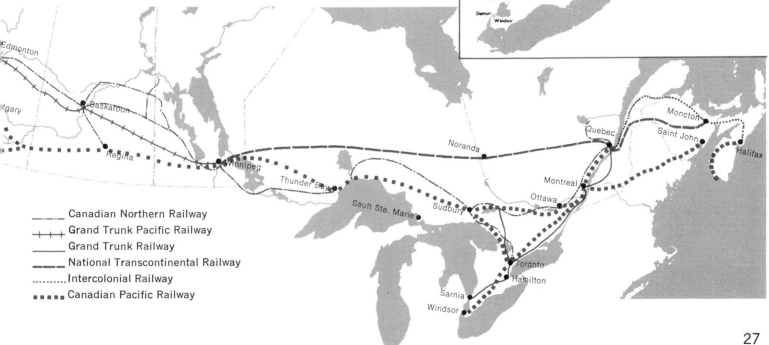

_._._._ Canadian Northern Railway
+++ Grand Trunk Pacific Railway
_____ Grand Trunk Railway
_ _ _ National Transcontinental Railway
.... Intercolonial Railway
▪▪▪▪ Canadian Pacific Railway

At this time, the people we now call Ukrainians were referred to in Canada as Austrians, Galicians, Bukovinians, Ruthenians, Little Russians, Southainians, and sometimes Gallatians.

Find out why the Ukrainians were known by so many names.

Outdoor bake oven

Church-going in a Western town

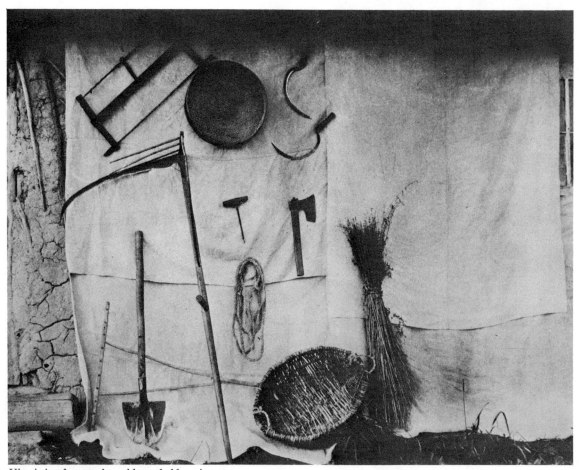

Ukrainian farm tools and household equipment

Breaking newly cleared ground

Doctor Joseph Oleskow, a Ukrainian from Lemburg, Austria, wrote this letter to the Canadian Department of the Interior on March 16, 1895.

A great number of Galician agriculturists of Ruthenian (Slavic) nationality desire to quit their native country, due to over-population, subdivision of land holdings, heavy taxation, and unfavourable political conditions.

The question therefore arises to find a country with ample good, free land for settlement, willing to accept thousands of farmers,—who although possessed of modest means, are diligent and thrifty—and to offer them the opportunity to attain a decent subsistence.

The representatives of the Brazilian Government are conducting intensive propaganda with the aim of directing the flow of emigration towards Brazil, . . .

The Committee of the prospective emigrant farmers has decided to make enquiries about the possibilities offered to agriculturists wishing to settle in Canada. . . .

The writer would come to Canada in order to survey places suitable for mass-settlement of emigrants.

Begging to be excused for not having the courage to use my inadequate knowledge of English to be able to write this letter,

> *I remain,*
> > *Very truly yours,*
> > *[Signed] J. Oleskow*

1. Why were these Galicians or Ukrainians anxious to leave their own country?
2. What is the major reason for Mr. Oleskow's letter?

3. In what other country are the Ukrainians considering settlement? Why? Which country, Canada or Brazil, has a climate more like that of the countries from which the Ukrainians plan to emigrate?

Later in 1895, Dr. Oleskow wrote a pamphlet, *About Free Lands,* to inform the Ukrainians about conditions in Canada.

If someone finishes public school there, he is an educated person and may be elected to any office. . . .

The climate varies in different parts of Canada; in the provinces where there is free land available, the climate is very much like that of our country, only the winters are as a rule more severe. . . . There are all kinds of roads (in Canada) and much money is spent for their construction. . . . Railways are everywhere where settlements are situated. This is simply because railways are built first and people settle along the lines afterwards. . . .

The whole country is divided into squares, sections of 640 acres each. A settler and his family, or a single man over 18 years of age, can obtain a quarter of such a section. Each section has a number. Along the railway lines on both sides of them to a depth of 4 miles, odd-numbered sections belong to railway companies.

Colonist sleeping cars

In less-densely populated parts of the country they are sold at $3 per acre, with 10 years to complete the payments. Even-numbered sections belong to the government, and are given away as homesteads. . . .

The settler receives the patent of ownership after three years, provided he can prove that he was residing on the land at least 6 months each year, that he built a house, and that he has brought under cultivation a certain amount of land. . . .

The crossing of the ocean lasts one week, and travel by rail in Europe and in Canada takes about 5 days. Inexperienced people are not advised to venture alone. It is best to travel in groups under the guidance of an experienced person who knows the language, or who can at least speak German. . . .

In order to make a living on the land given to them, one should have enough money to be able to live after arrival until the next crop is garnered, to be able to buy a pair of oxen for ploughing, as well as implements for husbandry, or at least enough ready money to be able to hire a neighbour of longer standing to do the ploughing. The first settlers who emigrate must also have a few hundred florins in cash for the upkeep of their families. Those who arrive after them may be able to manage with less money, working on arrival for wages with farmers who came before them, and later, when they have acquired some knowledge of the language, they can be hired by other farmers. After a year they will earn so much cash that they will be able to take out their own homestead. . . .

The best time to emigrate to Canada is in the early spring, because this will enable the settler to put in some potatoes and to sow some grain on his ploughed acres. Towards the summer, only those who intend to work during harvest time to earn some additional money to start farming should emigrate. Nobody should venture to Canada in the late autumn or early winter, because he will have difficulty in finding work and will have to spend his money, perhaps his last cent, to live through the winter. . . .

**1. This pamphlet was written before Oleskow visited Canada. Do you think he gave an accurate picture to Ukrainians of life in Canada?
2. What time of year does he encourage settlers to come to Canada? Why? Suppose due to unforeseen circumstances you arrived in the fall. What would you need to bring with you in order to survive until the spring? From whom might you expect help?**

Mykailo Stashyn was one member of a party of Ukrainians who came to Canada in 1896. As you read his report, compare his description with that of Dr. Oleskow before he came to Canada.

After two weeks' stay in Winnipeg, we were taken to Stuartburn some sixty miles south of Winnipeg. We were brought to the big farm of a man who was raising stock, and he allowed us to use his stables as our temporary dwellings. We slept indoors, but all housework was done outdoors. There the laundry was washed, the bread was baked, the meals were cooked, and we, the children, played near our mothers. Our fathers went to select homesteads with the surveyors and to cut the lanes, because all land was covered with bush.

As soon as a homestead was measured, one of the heads of the families registered it in his name. All wanted to have as much wood on their land as possible. And that was because in the old country everybody was fed up with having to pay—or to work hard for the landlord in lieu of pay—for the privilege of obtaining some wood.

Everybody was asking the agent to allot homesteads as near as possible to each other. All wished to be with their friends, because being in a strange country, among strange people, whose language they could not understand, made them feel very lonely. . . .

Our father brought approximately $50 with him. Immediately on arrival he bought a cow so as to have milk for the children . . . He paid $22 for her. She was a very good cow, and gave enough milk to supply seven families.

After some time we moved onto our homestead in the bush to live. The cow used to go into the woods to graze and when milking time approached she came home on her own. It would seem that she was good and gracious to us, for we would have never been able to find her if we had had to look for her in the woods.

There were no roads worthy of that name, only trails. But even they had to be marked off with sticks, and we cut notches on trees so as not to lose our way to the next neighbour. In those days people were very friendly to each other. Visitors were received with open arms and accorded openhearted hospitality. They assisted each other in every way. This helped us to endure the hardships of pioneering and to overcome homesickness.

The time came to build the house as winter was approaching. But how does one build a house? Nykola Genik stood us in good stead. He hailed from the Carpathian Mountains and knew how to build shacks. He helped us put up our house. It wasn't much of a house. A ditch three feet deep was dug, and two poles in each end of the ditch were put in, with a log across. Long poplar poles were then leaned to on the log and covered with sod. The end walls were plastered with clay. In one a pane of glass 10" x 10" was put in, and in the other a door made from hewn poplar planks. It

Chinese grocery

was a memorable day when we moved into our own house. There was great rejoicing and great delight.

The banks of the walls served us as beds. An old ink bottle was used as a lamp to light the house in the evenings. The fuel did not cost much. The lamp consumed only one quart of kerosene during the whole winter. We made wicks from threads.

We also accepted lodgers into our house. . . .

1. Find similarities and differences in the reports of Stashyn and Oleskow.
2. Why do these new settlers want their homesteads close together? Does this happen today with immigrants coming to Canada? Why do you think a downtown section of Toronto is known as ''Little Italy''? Are there any ethnic areas in your community?
3. Make a sketch of the exterior and interior of the first home described in Stashyn's report?

Ukrainian Orthodox Church, Manitoba

Compare your sketch with these two pictures of early prairie homes.

In the summer of 1898, the Commissioner of Immigration sent Leon Roy to determine the **progress** made by the Ukrainian **settlers** at Stuartburn:

In accordance with your instructions, on the 8th of August (1898) I proceeded to Stuartburn settlement, and when there I located twenty families on land as per list herewith attached. I have visited one hundred and forty Galician settlers, and find that the number of acres they have broken (i.e., new land broken)

are 39½
Under wheat 47½
Under oats 24
Under barley 30
Rye 2½
Under vegetables 77
Number of milk cows 128
Number of young cattle, working oxen and horses 234
Number of poultry 1084

34

These 146 families have cheap, but very comfortable houses. Their building improvements on each place are worth at an average about $50.00. Plenty of hay put for their stock. The growing crop is good, and seems well put in, except the potatoes that are poor. Plenty of work to be had in the neighborhood of the settlement, and they ought to be able to make enough to support themselves during the coming winter.

1. **Why do you suppose the Ukrainians have been so successful?**

2. **Make a list of the reasons why each of the groups we have examined decided to leave their own country, why they chose to immigrate to Canada, how they travelled to Canada, what problems they faced once they arrived here, and what were the advantages of coming to Canada rather than remaining in their own country. What contributions have they made to Canadian life?**

Discrimination in Canadian Immigration Policy?

The immigrants we have looked at so far had been welcomed by the Canadian government. Did Canada always have this "open door" policy towards immigrants from all countries and of all races?

INVESTIGATION 1

During the building of the government-sponsored railroad in the early 1880s, many labourers were required. To meet the need for cheap and plentiful labour, many Chinese were encouraged to come to Canada to assist in this significant national endeavour. The following paragraph indicates some of the problems encountered when Chinese labourers were brought to Canada to help build the railroad.

From *Blazing the Trail Through the Rockies,* by Noel Robinson:
Onderdonk [contractor for the B.C. line of the C.P.R.] found the white labour that he had got from San Francisco—the only source of supply at the moment—consisted for the most part of clerks out of employment, broken-down bartenders and other of that ilk, men who had never handled a shovel before and who often appeared on the scene attired in fashionable garments in a rather tattered state, who might even be seen in the cuttings with patent leather shoes, much the worse for wear and trousers sprung over the foot. So he determined to import a lot of Chinamen . . . and he got two ship loads, 1,000 men each. They came in very bad weather and had to be kept below hatches most of the way, so as soon as they got upon the work and began to take violent exercise, they developed scurvy and were decimated, fully one-tenth of their number dying. Being fatalists, as soon as a man was stricken with scurvy the others would not wait upon him or even give him a drink, and the government agent at Yale had great difficulty in getting them buried when they died. In fact many of their bodies were so lightly covered with a few rocks and a little earth that one became unpleasantly aware of the fact while walking along the line.

1. List some of the difficulties encountered by the Chinese.
2. Examine the cartoon shown on this page and give reasons why Chinese immigrants were not given the same kind of reception as their European counterparts.
3. Amor de Cosmos, Premier of British Columbia, seems to be treating Chinese labourers very unfairly after their contribution to the building of the C.P.R, Some people would call this an example of racial prejudice. What does this term mean? Can you cite other examples?

INVESTIGATION 2

There was a time, only six decades ago, when Americans—of all people!—found themselves in a position to accuse Canadians of race prejudice. In 1970, liberal Canadians are quick to apply the word "racist" to American society, and no doubt with justice. But in the early years of this century, when Canada's character was being formed, newspapers in Washington and Chicago charged that Canada was officially anti-Negro. For in those years the Canadian government consciously and carefully applied a policy of nearly total exclusion of American blacks. This is why Canada today has comparatively few blacks, why it is still possible for us to think of race problems as things that happen to other people.

It is not a pleasant chapter in our history. It involves no boldly stated policy of the kind that goes into the school textbooks. There was nothing public about it, as with the "Keep Australia White" policy. Rather it was a back-room effort, almost entirely successful, to "discourage" the many thousands of American and West Indian blacks who might otherwise have moved to Canada. There was—as government correspondence in Ottawa records now makes clear—a long, long series of letters exchanged among immigra-

tion authorities worried about how to be functionally anti-black without *seeming* anti-black.

The policy goes back at least to 1898, the year when W. D. Scott became superintendent in Clifford Sifton's department of immigration. He was to hold that position for twenty-two years, and to func-

tion for that period as the most important interpreter, on the daily working level, of Canada's immigration policies.

In those years Canada, and particularly the Canadian West, looked inviting to many American blacks. Canada had a pre-Civil War reputation as the end of the Underground

Railroad, where escaped slaves could find safety. Many American blacks were discovering that even in the North they were discriminated against. They wanted, the evidence shows, to go to Canada, get some of that free land the Canadians were offering, and set up as farmers.

Canada didn't want them, and didn't get them. In the period 1896-1907, when 1.3 million Europeans and Americans became Canadian immigrants, less than nine hundred blacks were admitted.

The reasons were never clear, but certainly there were plenty of reasons given. Canadian officials tended to think blacks were poor farmers, were perhaps immoral, were generally undesirable immigrants; above all, it was repeated again and again that black people couldn't stand the cold.

From *Saturday Night* Magazine, Sept. 1970

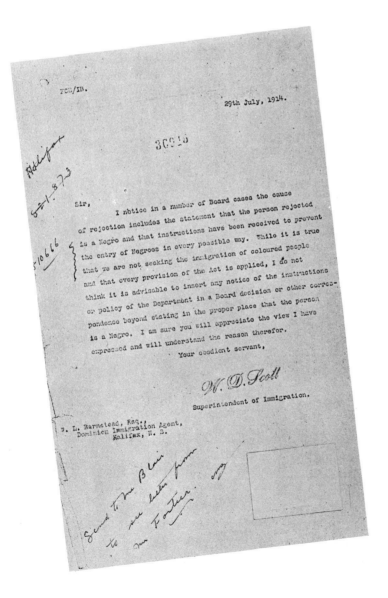

1. Do you think that the reasons for not admitting Negroes to Canada were good ones, or were they reasons behind which to hide prejudice towards the Negro?
2. Was our anti-Negro immigration policy proclaimed in law? How then was it enforced? Why do you think that it was never written down?

INVESTIGATION 3

Between March 4 and October 31, 1942, more than 21,000 men, women, and children of Japanese ancestry were evacuated from their homes on the coast of British Columbia. Three quarters of these people were Canadian-born, and many of the others were naturalized citizens. But citizen and alien were treated alike. Canada's declaration of war on Japan immediately after Pearl Harbor on December 7, 1941, only partially explains the mass removal of the Japanese-Canadians; Canada was also at war with Germany and Italy but no such action was taken against Canadians of German or Italian ancestry.

Japanese immigrants first came to British Columbia in any numbers in 1884. Within a few years, they encountered the same discrimination, such as disenfranchisement and restrictions on employment, as already affected the province's Chinese population. At the turn of the century, the provincial government tried to prevent a further influx of Oriental immigrants by passing an act that required intending immigrants to demonstrate an ability to read the act in some European language. Six times between 1900 and 1908 the Legislature passed the act. On five occasions, the federal government disallowed the legislation because it conflicted with an Anglo-Japanese treaty; on one occasion, the lieutenant-governor reserved it.

Between 1905 and 1908, almost 12,000 Japanese, of whom 90 percent were adult males, entered Canada, and most of them remained in British Columbia. This rapid influx of Japanese stimulated the 1907 organization of the Asiatic Exclusion League in Vancouver. The league soon had a membership of over 2,000, including businessmen, labour leaders, and representatives of both the Conservative and Liberal Parties. In September, 1907, a league-sponsored parade got out of hand, developed into a riot, and resulted in extensive damage to both the Chinese and Japanese sections of the city.

The continued growth of the Japanese population by natural increase and by immigration rankled British Columbians, who began to agitate for the total exclusion of Japanese immigrants

Nov. 11

Listening once long ago to an
Old man in Slocan saying
"You can trust 'em if ther white,"
And I piping up—I was a spunky
*   eight—*
"Can't you trust me? I was born in
Canada. I'm Canadian." And
He not looking but talking
About bratty jap kids with
Snotty noses—mine wasn't—
And always, come Nov. 11
I remember all those who
Sacrificed their ears for war.

Joy Kogawa

through a measure similar to the Chinese Immigration Act of 1923. Such an act of exclusion against Japanese was politically impossible, but the Japanese government agreed to impose further restrictions on emigrants. In 1928, the Japanese government agreed to permit no more than 150 Japanese of any class to emigrate to Canada in any one year. Japan lived up to this obligation, but the Japanese population of British Columbia continued to grow.

In Canada, the Oriental problem was unique to British Columbia; over 90 percent of the Japanese and 60 percent of the Chinese in Canada resided in British Columbia. British Columbia was the part of Canada nearest to the Orient, and most immigrants could not afford to travel further inland. British Columbia, with its economy based on primary industries of lumbering, mining, and fishing, offered employment opportunities to unskilled and semiskilled workers. Provincial legislation, however, was gradually imposed on the employment of Asians in these industries, and forced them into agriculture, retailing, and the service industries.

From *Documentary Problems in Canadian History* edited by J. M. Bumstead, pp. 215-16.

Japanese labourers from Honolulu

1. If you had been living in British Columbia at this time and Japan had suddenly attacked your ally, would you have felt uneasy with so many Japanese living in your country?
2. Do you think the Canadian government was justified in removing all Japanese, even those who were Canadian citizens, from their homes and placing them in special camps?
3. Why was it the Japanese alone rather than the Italians, Japanese, and Germans that the government removed from their homes? Was the Asian problem new to British Columbia?
4. Do you think that this same type of situation could ever arise again in Canada?

Canadians are often smug and quick to blame other countries for discrimination without ever realizing or admitting our own prejudices. This quiz might make us realize our own blindness.

QUIZ

Answer the following questions as honestly as possible. On a separate piece of paper mark *yes, no,* or *uncertain* after each question.

1. Do you like cats? Answer *yes, no,* or *uncertain.*

2. Do you like raw oysters? Answer *yes, no,* or *uncertain.*

3. Do you like classical music? Answer *yes, no,* or *uncertain.*

4. Would you like to live in Europe? Answer *yes, no,* or *uncertain.*

5. Do you like to waltz? Answer *yes, no,* or *uncertain.*

6. Would you like to know what is in this package?

On a new piece of paper answer the following questions.

1. Have you ever owned a cat for more than a month? *Yes* or *No.*

2. Have you ever eaten raw oysters? *Yes* or *No.*

3. Have you ever attended a symphony or listened to a complete recording of one? *Yes* or *No.*

4. Have you ever been to Europe? *Yes* or *No.*

5. Do you know how to waltz? *Yes* or *No.*

6. Do you think there is something valuable in this package. Answer *yes, no,* or *uncertain.*

Place both sets of your answers side by side. Here is how you score the test.

1. You get a zero if the second part of the question was answered *no* and the first part was answered either *yes* or *no.*
E.g., Do you like cats? *Yes.* (Or *No*)
Have you ever owned a cat for more than a month? *No.*

2. You get one point if you answered the second part of the question *yes* and the first part either *yes* or *no.*
E.g., Do you like cats? *Yes.* (Or *No*)
Have you ever owned a cat for more than a month? *Yes.*

3. You get two points if you answered the second part of the question *no* and answered the first part *uncertain.*
E.g., Do you like cats? *Uncertain.*
Have you ever owned a cat for more than a month? *No.*

4. You get three points if you answered the second part of the question *yes* and the first part of the question *uncertain.*
E.g., Do you like cats? *Uncertain.*
Have you ever owned a cat for more than a month? *Yes.*

Each pair of questions is scored in this way, except for the last question regarding the box. Regardless of how you answer the first part of the last question, you receive a zero if you answer either *yes* or *no* to the second part and three points if you answer *uncertain*. (The question was: "Do you think there is something valuable in this package?")

This is how you rate:

15-18—very open-minded, honest, willing to study the facts

14-18—average

9-5—below average, likely to jump to conclusions, prone to prejudice

4-0—very prone to prejudice, easily influenced by opinion of others, or by externals

Discussion of Prejudice

1. Can you really judge something if you have had little or no experience of it? Can you judge the taste of an oyster by its appearance? The beauty of music without seriously listening to it?

2. You have probably heard a statement like this: "I love kittens but I can't stand cats." I think if I were a cat I would resent it because it indicates a prejudgment of all cats. Can you think of any other similar clichés, but ones which deal with people, for example, the American Indian? What effect if any do such statements have on a person who has never met an Indian? Are you aware of having formed any judgments about a group of people based not on personal contact but on such slogans?

3. Jumping to conclusions based on first impressions or on the hearsay evidence of a friend is rather common. Is it a good habit? Can you think of possible dangers in it? What is the difference between taking a friend's word for something—that is, trust—and being gullible?

4. Is forming rash conclusions illogical? When isn't it illogical? Is it a good habit?

5. What's the difference between forming a rash conclusion about oysters or cats and doing the same thing to a person? What do we usually call such a rash, unfounded judgment of a person?

6. If you decided that the box contained something valuable or useless, what prompted your decision? Was it a logical decision or a hunch? What's the difference between a hunch and a prejudice?

7. People are like boxes; they all have different wrappings but we can never be sure what is inside them until they open up. Is it a kind of prejudice to judge a person before you get to know what's inside him? How often do person's wrappings actually indicate what's inside?

8. We don't mind if a person makes a bad judgment so long as he is willing to change his mind when he is proven wrong. What happens when he refuses—or when he can't change his mind? What do you do then?

9. From the quiz we have just done we can see that just about all of us are at least slightly prone to prejudice. Just what is prejudice in your opinion?

10. What would be the opposite of prejudice? How can you develop the habit of "not being prejudiced"?

From *Self-Awareness Through Group Dynamics* by Richard Reichert

The Future of Immigration in Canada

Here is a problem that is presently facing Canada with regard to immigration. Should Canada be accepting large numbers of immigrants at a time when there are not enough jobs for Canadians? Here is what Joseph Sedgwick thinks:

Let Canada reach top population naturally by limiting immigration, Sedgwick suggests

Toronto lawyer Joseph Sedgwick suggested yesterday that a better alternative to letting large numbers of people from other lands into Canada might be to ascertain an optimum population for the nation and allow it to be reached by natural increase in births.

"We owe no debt that I am aware of to the people who want to come here," he told the mid-winter meeting of the Canadian Bar Association. "We should admit them only if we need them.

"It may well be, that in our present condition, and with the unemployment rate that we now have, some 20 to 25 millions of people is the optimum population for Canada, and that we do not need any more backs to shoulder our burden."

Mr. Sedgwick has twice examined immigration for the federal Government—once five years ago when he inquired into the problem of deserting seamen and again in 1970 when he was asked to report on the increasing number of non-immigrants applying for permanent residence.

In his speech yesterday, he dismissed as a cliche the traditional concept of Canada as a vast, empty land that could support, he said, "God knows how many people—depending on who was talking or sometimes on how much land he or his company had for sale.

"Sure, we still have millions of acres with a negligible population but many of those acres can never support more than a marginal population.

"No amount of industry will make the Laurentian shield into a wheat field or a pasture, nor will the greatest endeavor convert the muskeg in the North into anything other than what it is."

He said it may now be time to take a sober second look at immigration.

"Maybe, instead of blindly encouraging people to come to this land of opportunity, we should make a serious study, ecological and demological, to find out just how many people each region can reasonably support, and just what at this time is in the best interest of the people who are now in Canada.

"It may be that natural increase would cause us to reach that desirable figure without any immigration at all."

Mr. Sedgwick said that Canada might profitably devote more time to the problem of emigration, which results in the annual loss of thousands of Canada's best-trained and best-educated citizens. "May we not think less of making Canada an attractive place to come to and more of making it an attractive place in which to remain."

The Globe and Mail, Toronto, Feb. 6, 1972

Canada is a country with vast lands and relatively few people. Do we owe a debt to the overpopulated countries of the world by allowing some of their surplus people to immigrate to Canada? Or, should we, as Mr. Sedgwick suggests, close our doors and let our population increase only by birth from within our country?

The Contributions of Our Immigrants

Immigrants have contributed more than their strength to building the railways or their skills in various professions.

1. What country did the popular "Canadian" sport of curling come from? The clue is in the players' hats. 2. List the examples pictured on this page of the richness and variety added to Canadian life by immigrants and find as many other instances as you can.

Costumes, music, dances, sports, customs, languages, religions, and even foods have been contributed from countries around the world to add to the wealth of the Canadian mosaic.

Curling in 1875

Schnitzing bee, Mennonite women at Kitchener, Ontario

The Chinese
art of fencing

Judo club, Toronto

These menus appeared recently at banquets. Try to discover from which country each recipe was brought to Canada. On a map of the world draw arrows from the country of origin to Canada. Can you discover any other dishes introduced to Canada that do not appear here?

1
French Onion Soup
Weiner Schnitzel,
Welsh Rarebit, or
Irish Stew
Revani (Greek Glazed Cake)
Greek Easter Bread

2
Scotch Broth
Curried Lamb,
Ragout of Duck, or
Coq au Vin
Apple Strudel
French Bread

3
Potato Soup
Beef Stroganoff,
Buffalo Sukiyaki, or
Ravioli
Swedish Tea Rings
Mandel Bread
Mary's Polish Bread

4
Mushroom Soup
Sweet and Sour Spareribs
Holubuse (Ukrainian for
Cabbage Rolls)
Quiche Lorraine
Trifle
Scotch Graham Scones and
Seville Marmalade
Dutch Kringle Bread

5
Cheese Soup
Beef and Kidney Pie
or Tortiere
Dutch Speculas
Pousse Cafe
Hot Cross Buns

6
Split Pea Soup
Hungarian Goulash
or Chicken Cacciatore
Charlotte Russe
Hungarian Coffee Cake

How wide does Canada intend to open its door?

Can Canada afford to be the only industrial country in the world readily open to immigrants from Third World developing countries?

How fast will computers make obsolete the routine, low-skill jobs at the bottom of the economic structure?

What is the ideal population for Canada: 25 million, 30 million, 50 million?

Will immigrants in the Seventies be willing to wait nearly a generation, as their predecessors did, for integration into Canadian life?

These are the kind of tough questions raised by a shift in Canadian immigration policy to make access easier for low-skill immigrants.

It is not clear how far the open-door policy will go. A lot will depend on public reaction when its effects start becoming more visible, probably in the fall, but Immigration Minister Bryce Mackasey has made it clear that he personally favors easier entry.

His basic thesis, outlined in a recent interview, is that despite current economic problems and unemployment there is still room for a larger number of low-skill workers at the bottom of the Canadian social structure.

As education levels rise in Canada, he said, more and more Canadians are reluctant to do low-skill, low-status jobs and immigrants will have to be brought in to do them.

Canada's experience with large-scale immigration has been good, he said. There is no reason to fear it now. This essentially traditionalist view of immigration has many supporters among economic experts. Others fear it will create serious social problems with which Canada is not ready to deal.

Does Canada need more unskilled immigrants?

Economists disagree on short-term needs; generally agree that in the long term, as Canada moves from industrialism to post-industrialism, low-skill jobs will become redundant as such trends as computerization quicken.

Don't want jobs

For the short term, some economists agree with Mr. Mackasey that there are low-status slots going unfilled because Canadians don't want them. Others say Canada should slow immigration and allow the population to achieve its optimum by natural growth. There is, predictably, little agreement on what is the optimum.

Mr. Mackasey believes Canada should have 50 million people to provide a large domestic market and enable the economy to become more independent of the United States.

Other economists say this kind of thinking is pipe-dreaming. Their view is that the economy will be decided in the United States.

After the end of the Vietnam war, the U.S. economy is likely to need drastic streamlining and one effect they predict is a trend pushing Canada into a resource-producing role. The resource industries will need increasingly less labor and in any case, these economists argue, liberal policies make it impossible to forcibly direct new immigrants to where they are most needed.

What have other industrial countries done?

The three main countries receiving immigrants—the United States, Britain and Australia—have put up barriers to low-skill immigration while generally remaining in the world-wide chase for the top layer of the "brain and professional" sector.

The main effect of the barriers is to block immigrants from the underdeveloped to the developed world although the barriers are usually erected on grounds of skill rather than color or racial origin.

Only the Australian policy openly discriminates on racial grounds, since it allows easy entry to any Commonwealth citizen of "European origin": a provision that would enable a white Canadian to enter Australia regardless of his skills but would force a Canadian Indian to make a more difficult application like a non-Commonwealth citizen.

For non-Commonwealth immigration, job skills are a key factor and the barriers are aimed at preventing large-scale colored immigration from India and Asia.

What was the much-talked-of immigration backlog?

It was made up mainly of people who came to Canada as visitors then applied to settle, were refused, but stayed to fight the refusal.

When a visitor applies to stay he must normally score 50 points on a 90-point scale awarded for language, education and job skills and general suitability for life in Canada as assessed by an immigration officer. If he is turned down, the applicant can ask for a special inquiry to review the first officer's decision. If the inquiry officer turns him down, he is ordered deported but he can still stay and wait to go before an Immigration Appeal Board.

Thousands waiting

By June, 1972, there were 13,500 waiting for special inquiries and another 10,000 waiting for appeal boards.

What did the Government do about the backlog?

The 13,500 waiting for special inquiries will shortly receive letters inviting them to submit evidence of their integration into Canadian life for a review. The review will have its comic side, since official secret directives have been sent to immigration officers ordering them to seek evidence in favor of the applicant—any evidence, however slender, including having opened a bank account or joined a church or ethnic club.

One senior Ottawa official summarized the position like this: "The name of the game is to clear the backlog—we are really going to try all out to grant landed status to everyone." ➞

Why was the backlog a political embarrassment?

The ethnic vote is a much debated issue; no one is sure if it exists or what it does but most politicians play it safe and assume they must court voters as members of ethnic groups.

Some feel unsure

Several Liberal members in Toronto are known to feel shaky in their ridings and the Liberal caucus is aware of the need to do everything that will strengthen these seats.

Most of the backlog was in Toronto and a sympathetic approach was considered worthwhile, particularly since the alternative—mass deportations—was politically unthinkable.

How will the backlog situation affect the future?

In theory they are not connected, but in practice they are. It makes no kind of political sense to clear one backlog and let another one build up. Officially, streamlined procedures will prevent a new backlog but this statement is generally taken with a large pinch of salt.

Mr. Mackasey has instructed his officers to interpret the points system leniently by, for example, awarding points more readily for personality or language skills or education. This will make entry easier without changing the law, but the key issue is how far the leniency will go.

Up to the day of the announcement about clearing the backlog (June 3), directives were going out ordering a wide open-door policy for new immigrants as well as for people in the backlog. But sensing that a major controversy was likely to break out, the minister pulled back at the last minute.

Now, official policy is that arrivals after June 3 will benefit from a lenient interpretation of the points system but not the special leniency to be applied to the backlog.

The Globe and Mail, Toronto, July 12, 1972

Backlog unwanted

But no one, least of all immigration officers, believes the Government will stand for the build-up of another backlog during an election year. They are sure that word will quickly circulate abroad that it will remain easier to settle in Canada by applying inside the country than going through the so-called normal procedures in their own countries, where there is no appeal against a turn-down.

1. After reading this article, do you agree with Mr. Mackasey that Canada should have an "open-door" policy towards immigrants from all countries and of all levels of job skills?

2. List the arguments for and against an open-door policy. Check with Mr. Sedgwick's opinions on page 43.

3. How do politics effect the present policy towards immigrants waiting appeals and those applying to come into Canada?

4. How will these recent policies affect immigration in the future?

5. You are the Minister of Manpower and Immigration. Devise an immigration policy that you feel Canada should promote in the 1970s.

6. Your father is out of work, yet the three older sons in an immigrant family that just moved to Canada have all gotten jobs. How do you feel about the situation? Would you make any adjustments to the immigration policy you have just devised? Would this adjustment be for the good of our country and of the overpopulated countries or would it just satisfy your immediate feelings?

7. In general, has immigration been good for the Canadian nation? Where would Canada be if no one had ever immigrated to this country?

8. List all the ways in which four different immigrant groups have contributed to Canadian society.

9. After considering all you have learned during your investigation of *Canada: Land of Immigrants,* what do you think should be Canada's immigration policy in the future? How will this affect the development of our nation?